T0015846

THE TOP TEN

MOST DANGEROUS DINOSAURS

WSKids
WHITE STAR KIDS

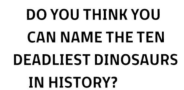

LET'S BEGIN!

DO YOU THINK YOU CAN NAME THE TEN DEADLIEST DINOSAURS IN HISTORY?

Surely you're imagining large carnivores, such as the T. rex. But did you know that brute force didn't always prevail? Sometimes an unsuspected secret weapon used at the right time could be more effective and destructive. So, even a peaceful herbivorous dinosaur could turn into **A DEADLY MACHINE!**

LETHAL WEAPON   **TRIVIA**

Look for these symbols to learn surprising **TRIVIA** and discover what **LETHAL WEAPONS** made these **TEN DINOSAURS** worthy of our ranking!

THE DANGER LEVEL WILL INCREASE AS WE GO FROM **TEN** ALL THE WAY UP TO TERRIBLE NUMBER **ONE!**

WARNING!
At the bottom of the page you'll find the names of the **TEN DINOSAURS** on our list. Try to guess their ranking by writing their names on the lines below.
AS YOU READ THE BOOK, YOU'LL FIND OUT HOW MANY YOU GUESSED RIGHT!

1 _____

2 _____

3 _____

4 _____

5 _____

6 _____

7 _____

8 _____

9 _____

10 _____

I'm not part of the top ten, but keep reading to discover exactly who (and what) I am!

- STEGOSAURUS
- APATOSAURUS
- TRICERATOPS

- T. REX
- IGUANODON
- ANKYLOSAURUS

- THERIZINOSAURUS
- DEINONYCHUS
- TROODON
- SPINOSAURUS

10. IGUANODON

SCIENTIFIC NAME:
Iguanodon bernissartensis

LENGTH: 43 ft (13 m)

It may have looked like easy prey, but it was all a trick to fool unsuspecting predators. In fact, if attacked, Iguanodon would have used its **LARGE, SOLID CLAWS** (which were actually like thumbnails) to defend itself. When it wasn't being threatened, it used those same claws to bring leaf-rich branches closer to its mouth. When it came to one-on-one combat, those deadly spikes became **DAGGERS** to be driven into the chest of the attacker, who would then soon give up.

ESTIMATED WEIGHT: 3-4 tons (3-4 metric tons)

DIET: herbivore (plant-eater)

PERIOD: Cretaceous (125 million years ago)

LETHAL WEAPON
Large spiked claws
on its thumbs.

TRIVIA
Its name means
"iguana-tooth."

STEGOSAURUS

SCIENTIFIC NAME:
Stegosaurus ungulatus

LENGTH: 30 ft (9 m)

What made this mellow dinosaur so threatening? After all, given the small size of its head, and thus its brain, it probably was not the sharpest knife in the drawer.

Its strength was concentrated in its tail, at the end of which were **LARGE, SHARP SPIKES**. Swinging its tail around, a blow from a Stegosaurus was so powerful that it could **BREAK THE SKULL** or legs of any predator bold enough to dare to attack it.

ESTIMATED WEIGHT: 7.7 tons (7 metric tons)

DIET:
herbivore
(plant-eater)

PERIOD:
Jurassic
(150 million years ago)

LETHAL WEAPON
Long, thick spikes
on its tail.

TRIVIA
Its brain was
slightly larger than a walnut.

8

THERIZINOSAURUS

SCIENTIFIC NAME:
Therizinosaurus cheloniformis

What? You've never heard of me?

LENGTH: 33 ft (10 m)

You can't help but be terrified when you see Therizinosaurus! In fact, its front limbs ended in **HUGE CLAWS** in the shape of **LONG SCYTHES**, up to 3.3 feet (1 m) long.

They were generally used to bring leafy branches (its favorite food) within reach. But if some large carnivore tried to turn Therizinosaurus into a tasty meal, those same claws would surely drive the predator away. In fact, even a small scratch from those claws could be lethal.

lbs ESTIMATED **WEIGHT:** 6.6 tons (6 metric tons)

DIET:
herbivore
(plant-eater)

? **PERIOD:**
Cretaceous
(70 million years ago)

LETHAL WEAPON
Hands with giant claws.

TRIVIA
The first Therizinosaurus fossils were discovered nearly 80 years ago in the Gobi Desert in Mongolia.

ANKYLOSAURUS

SCIENTIFIC NAME:
Ankylosaurus
magniventris

LENGTH: 30 ft (9 m)

Ankylosaurus's main **WEAPON OF DEFENSE** was its tough armor, which covered most of its body and head.
As tough as a tank, this dinosaur also had a tail that ended in a sort of **MACE WEIGHING NEARLY 110 LBS (50 KG)**, which it used like a wrecking ball. By spinning it in the air, it could accurately hit large predators (even a T. rex!) and shatter their leg bones.

 lbs

**ESTIMATED
WEIGHT:** 8.8 tons
(8 metric tons)

DIET:
herbivore
(plant-eater)

PERIOD:
Cretaceous
(70 million years ago)

LETHAL WEAPON
A heavy club
on the end of its tail.

TRIVIA
Even its eyes were protected
by small plates instead of eyebrows.

ARMORED DINOSAURS

ARMOR was definitely one of the most effective defense strategies. Preventing a predator's teeth and claws from reaching the most vulnerable parts of the body could mean the difference between life and death. If you then add SPIKES AND CLUBS as weapons to use against an attacker, well, you can easily see how dinosaurs such as Stegosaurus and Ankylosaurus, both of which had their own type of ARMOR, were able to ward off predators.

EVEN THE MOST CUNNING, FEROCIOUS CARNIVORES WOULD HAVE THOUGHT TWICE BEFORE ATTACKING LIVING "TANKS" LIKE ANKYLOSAURUS AND THE THREE ARMORED DINOSAURS SHOWN HERE.

Gastonia

Protected by its **JAW-BREAKING ARMOR**, Gastonia could go head-to-head with even the fierce Utahraptor! The Utahraptor could really get injured on the **SHARP STUDS** that lined Gastonia's armor and tail, as well as the **BIG SPIKES** on the shoulders of this herbivore. Unlike Ankylosaurus, its tail was not armed with a club.

Armor and spikes.

It was named in honor of U.S. amateur paleontologist Rob Gaston.

Cretaceous
(125 million years ago)

Sauropelta

Armor and spikes.

Leaf-shaped teeth,
suitable for slicing vegetation.

Cretaceous
(125 million years ago)

Being completely covered with **SPIKES AND STUDDED ARMOR**, Sauropelta was rather safe. On its neck, the most delicate part of its body, it also had additional protection: **TUSK-LIKE SPIKES** that blocked the bite of even the largest predators.

Kentrosaurus

Similar to Stegosaurus but smaller, Kentrosaurus had something extra: Flat armor plates ran down its neck and part of its back, turning into long spikes on its hindquarters and tail. **PROTECTING ITS SHOULDERS** were two more extra-long **SPIKES**.

Very long spikes
on its body and
tail.

A flexible neck made it possible for this dinosaur to look over its shoulders.

Jurassic
(152 million years ago)

DEINONYCHUS

SCIENTIFIC NAME:
Deinonychus antirrhopus

Pretty feathers, aren't they?

LENGTH: 11.5 ft (3.5 m)

More than its size, what's impressive about this dinosaur is its hunting technique. Instead of chasing its prey, it preferred to lie in **AMBUSH** and assault unsuspecting prey, often from above, for example, by jumping down from a boulder or the branch of a tree. **THE SHARP, ROUNDED CLAW ON ITS HIND FEET,** 6 inches (15 cm) long, was probably used to hold its victims still on the ground. When it walked or ran, the claw was lifted upward toward its leg to prevent it from breaking against stones or other hard objects.

ESTIMATED WEIGHT: 220 lbs (100 kg)

DIET: carnivore (meat-eater)

PERIOD: Cretaceous (115 million years ago)

LETHAL WEAPON
A sharp curved claw on both feet.

TRIVIA
It was probably covered in feathers like birds.

MODERN DINOSAURS

Although their name means "terrible lizards," dinosaurs are more closely related to birds. In fact, some people consider birds to be **LIVING DINOSAURS**. However, unlike most birds today, dinosaurs couldn't fly. The shorter feathers served as a warm coat, while the longer feathers on their forelimbs allowed them to jump and then **GLIDE THROUGH THE AIR**.

THE TRANSFORMATION OF DINOSAURS INTO BIRDS HAS TAKEN A VERY LONG TIME AND HAS INVOLVED MANY NOW-EXTINCT INTERMEDIARY SPECIES THAT WERE AS DANGEROUS AS THEIR ANCESTORS. BUT SOME OF THE SPECIES ALIVE TODAY ARE PRETTY FEROCIOUS TOO! LET'S COMPARE TWO "BIRDS" FROM THE PAST WITH ONE FROM THE PRESENT.

Utahraptor

The lethality of the powerful Utahraptor is beyond question, given its large size, its **LONG CLAWS,** which were over 8 inches (20 cm) long, and its sharp **RAZOR-LIKE TEETH**. Utahraptor moved fast and in packs, terrorizing other dinosaurs.

Speed and claws.

It's likely that, at least when young, this dinosaur had feathers.

Cretaceous
(125 million years ago)

Terror Birds

In the Cenozoic era, flightless Terror Birds as tall as ostriches roamed the land. They inspired panic among small mammals, which they would grab with the claws on their wings. They would then bring their prey up to **THEIR ENORMOUS HOOKED BEAK,** using it to crush their **BONES.**

Intelligence and collaboration.

They were very fast runners thanks to their long, muscular legs.

Miocene
(23-5 million years ago)

Cassowary

Cassowaries have inherited the intense ferocity of their ancient ancestors. Though they're unable to fly, they're considered **THE MOST DANGEROUS BIRD** in the world because of the claws on their feet, which are 4 inches (10 cm) long. Able to kick with surprising force, they can easily take on anyone or anything they see as a threat.

Claws.

The male of the species is the one to brood and raise the chicks.

Present day

17

5

APATOSAURUS

● **SCIENTIFIC NAME:**
Apatosaurus ajax

LENGTH: 71 ft (21.5 m)

Its weight and enormous size alone were enough to make this **COLOSSAL HERBIVORE** completely unassailable. But woe to any beast that tried to hunt it, as they surely would have had to contend not only with the crushing power of its immense trunk-like legs, but also with its **LONG TAIL**. Very thin at the tip, it could be snapped like a **WHIP** at supersonic speeds and could even produce a frighteningly deafening **NOISE**, similar to a cannon shot.

ESTIMATED WEIGHT: 77 tons (70 metric tons)

lbs

DIET:
herbivore
(plant-eater)

PERIOD:
Jurassic
(150 million years ago)

Hey! From up here I can even see who's number 1!

LETHAL WEAPON
Its giant size
and whip-like tail.

TRIVIA
Its footprints were
more than 3.3 ft (1 m) wide.

PREHISTORIC GIANTS!

To defend themselves from predators, some herbivorous dinosaurs got bigger and bigger. You might even say they were **COLOSSAL**. Known as "long-necked dinosaurs," Sauropods were some the largest animals ever to walk on land. To appease their insatiable appetite, they would roam in groups in search of leaves, which they were able to reach thanks to their long necks.

ANYONE WHO ACCIDENTALLY ENDED UP NEAR THEIR FEET REALLY HAD TO LOOK OUT, AS THEY COULD EASILY BE SMASHED LIKE A PANCAKE. HERE ARE THREE OF THE BIGGEST SAUROPODS TO EVER EXIST.

Diplodocus

An adult Diplodocus was difficult to attack. When threatened, it could stand up on its hind legs and pounce on the predator with the full weight of its body, attempting to crush it. **THE SHARP CLAW ON ITS THUMB** could then deal a lethal blow.

Its size and thumb-claw.

Its eggs were round and as big as soccer balls.

Jurassic (154 million years ago)

Argentinosaurus

Its massive size.

It may have taken a lengthy 40 years to reach adulthood.

Cretaceous (94 million years ago)

Despite its considerable **LENGTH**, (estimated to be around 115 ft/35 m), Argentinosaurus was quite agile and relatively **FAST**. It probably had to defend itself against Giganotosaurus, a fierce predator that lived in the same area and possibly hunted in packs.

Brachiosaurus

Its massive size.

Its nostrils were on the top of its head so leaves wouldn't block its airways while eating.

In addition to a long flexible neck, Brachiosaurus had **FRONT LEGS THAT WERE LONGER** than its hind legs, meaning it could reach even the highest tree branches with ease, up to 30 ft (9 m) above ground.
Unlike other Sauropods, its tail was rather **SHORT**.

Jurassic (154 million years ago)

TRICERATOPS

SCIENTIFIC NAME:
Triceratops horridus

I thought I would be on the podium!

LENGTH: 30 ft (9 m)

The **HORNS** and the large bony collar of this dinosaur were certainly heavy, but Triceratops was probably glad to have them as they were necessary to its survival. As with today's bison, its large horns were used mainly in battles of strength between males, but they also came in handy if Triceratops was attacked by a large predator. If you then add its **POWERFUL MUSCLES,** it's easy to imagine how much fear it would have incited in those who happened to cross it!

 ESTIMATED WEIGHT: 8.8 tons (8 metric tons)

 DIET: herbivore (plant-eater)

 PERIOD: Cretaceous (66 million years ago)

You certainly deserve to be!

LETHAL WEAPON
Three horns and strong muscles.

TRIVIA
Its head measured 6.5 ft (2 m) in length and width.

T. REX

SCIENTIFIC NAME:
Tyrannosaurus rex

Third place?!
And to think that
I was once considered
the king!

LENGTH: 41 ft (12.5 m)

The T. rex was the ultimate predator! Its success can be credited to its immense, **TERRIFYING MOUTH**, lined with nearly 60 teeth that were always sharp because they were constantly being replaced by new ones.

T. rex preferred to eat live animals, but it wouldn't turn away from a carcass if it came across one. A highly developed sense of smell helped T. rex sniff out prey even from very far away. Once located, its victims hardly had a chance, given T. rex's incredibly **POWERFUL JAWS**—they were so strong they could easily have crushed a car!

ESTIMATED WEIGHT: 9.9 tons (9 metric tons)

DIET:
Carnivore
(meat-eater)

PERIOD:
Cretaceous
(68 million years ago)

LETHAL WEAPON
Teeth as long as bananas and a highly developed sense of smell.

TRIVIA
T. rex babies measured just under 3 feet (90 cm) long at birth, but grew very quickly.

LARGE CARNIVORES

The mightiest dinosaur predators walked by supporting their weight entirely on their powerful hind legs, while their **ARMS** were rather **SHORT**, though equipped with long claws. This let them run faster and move with greater agility than quadrupedal dinosaurs, which thus easily became their prey. All of them had **MASSIVE HEADS**, with mouths trimmed in a fearsome row of **TEETH**, which were often **JAGGED**.

THE SIZE OF SOME PREDATORS, SUCH AS THE THREE DEPICTED HERE, WAS IMPRESSIVE. THEIR LONG, STRONG TAILS WERE LIFTED OFF THE GROUND WHEN RUNNING TO BALANCE THE WEIGHT OF THEIR HEADS.

Carnotaurus

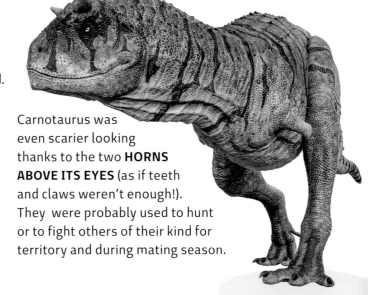

Sense of smell and speed.

Its hips were protected by stud-like plates.

Cretaceous
(70 million years ago)

Carnotaurus was even scarier looking thanks to the two **HORNS ABOVE ITS EYES** (as if teeth and claws weren't enough!). They were probably used to hunt or to fight others of their kind for territory and during mating season.

Giganotosaurus

Because of its considerable size, Giganotosaurus could scare even immense long-necked dinosaurs, like Argentinosaurus. With **MASSIVE JAWS**, it was able to cause **FATAL INJURIES**.

Big teeth and a powerful bite.

Its skull was up to 6 ft (1.8 m) long, but its brain was quite small.

Cretaceous (96 million years ago)

Tarbosaurus

You might think of Tarbosaurus as the Asian answer to T. rex. Like the T. rex, it had a **HUGE HEAD** and arms that were little more than bone. It preyed on large herbivores that it first separated from the herd and then caught by snapping them up in its jaws.

Big teeth and a powerful bite.

It could probably hear and smell better than it could see.

Cretaceous (70 million years ago)

SPINOSAURUS

SCIENTIFIC NAME:

Spinosaurus aegyptiacus

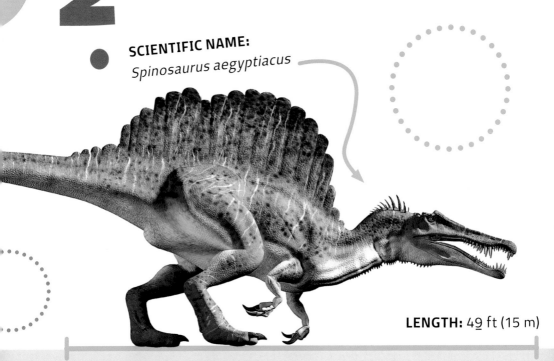

LENGTH: 49 ft (15 m)

Suffice it to say that Spinosaurus was, to date, the **LARGEST CARNIVORE** ever to have existed on Earth.

It caught prey, mostly fish, in large rivers, snapping them up with its claws and teeth, **LEAVING** them **NO WAY OUT**. In the water, it moved with agility, thanks to its **WEBBED FINGERS** and a tail tall enough to function as a **FIN** for swimming. The long "sail" on its back made it visible to all.

ESTIMATED WEIGHT: 7 tons (7 metric tons)

DIET: Carnivore (meat-eater)

PERIOD: Cretaceous (100 million years ago)

LETHAL WEAPON
A long crocodile-like snout
with lots of teeth.

TRIVIA
The first Spinosaurus fossils
ever discovered were destroyed
during WWII.

A SPECIAL DIET...

Sometimes it pays to choose unusual food, thereby avoiding fights with other predators over resources. That's exactly what the Spinosaurid family did: All members of this group loved to **EAT FISH!** They could eat other things too, and just like crocodiles today, if they happened to be in range, they would also nab land animals, including small dinosaurs.

LIKE HIPPOS, THEY HAD TO STAY SUBMERGED IN WATER FOR LONG PERIODS. THEY PROBABLY ALL HAD WEBBED FINGERS SO THAT THEY COULD SWIM BETTER. HERE ARE THREE "SPINY REPTILES."

Baryonyx

Baryonyx inhabited wetlands, where it had access to fresh water and fish at all times. Aside from having straight, longer legs, it must not have been much different than a **CROCODILE**. And it was probably just as **AGGRESSIVE**.

Conical teeth.

Its hips were protected by stud-like plates.

Cretaceous
(145 million years ago)

Suchomimus

A long snout with teeth.

The females would dig nests along riverbanks and lay up to 100 eggs.

Cretaceous (120 million years ago)

Scientists have discovered that Suchomimus had lighter bones than the rest of the family, which **PREVENTED IT FROM SUBMERGING UNDERWATER**. Thus it probably spent most of its time on land and looked for fish in shallow water.

Ichthyovenator

Ichthyovenator, meaning "fish hunter," is a name well-suited to this dinosaur. Like its relatives, it searched for prey in rivers, aided by **SPECIAL RECEPTORS** placed on its snout, which allowed it to find fish even in murky water.

Pressure receptors.

The sail on its back was split in two by a groove.

Cretaceous (125 million years ago)

TROODON

SURPRISE! I may be small, but I'm also the deadliest!

SCIENTIFIC NAME:
Troodon formosus

LENGTH: 6.5 ft (2 m)

Don't judge deadliness by appearance! Here we are, facing the **MOST INTELLIGENT** dinosaur ever to have existed—which also made it the most lethal.

Although it wasn't exactly gigantic, it was a skilled, successful hunter thanks to the attack strategies it implemented with its pack. Plus, it had an extra advantage: the **LARGE EYES AT THE FRONT OF ITS SKULL,** which made it possible to accurately calculate how far it was from its prey, even in the low light of dusk.

ESTIMATED WEIGHT: 88 lbs (40 kg)

DIET:
Carnivore (meat-eater)

PERIOD:
Cretaceous (75 million years ago)

LETHAL WEAPON
Intelligence
and teamwork.

TRIVIA
It laid eggs two by two, which is
why an even number of eggs are
always found in its nests.

SMART-OSAURUS!

The word "raptor" is used to refer to a group of dinosaurs that were not only **SIMILAR TO BIRDS**, but also **AGILE AND FAST**. Plus, they had **FEATHERS**, arms with **THREE LONG FINGERS**, **GOOD EYESIGHT**, and an extended, sharp **CLAW** on each foot. Raptors were generally small, about the size of a turkey, but some could be taller than a human.

THEY WERE ALL CLEVER PREDATORS. IN FACT, THEIR BRAINS WERE LARGER THAN THOSE OF OTHER DINOSAURS, ALTHOUGH SMALLER THAN THOSE OF MAMMALS. HERE ARE THREE EXAMPLES!

Microraptor

Similar to crows, dinosaurs in the Microraptor genus were covered in feathers. We even know the color: iridescent black. They had feathers on their arms and legs, which essentially made them an animal with **FOUR WINGS**.

The element of surprise and small teeth.

They used the claws of their hands and feet to climb tall trees, from which they would then jump down.

Cretaceous
(125 million years ago)

Velociraptor

Although covered in feathers from head to toe, species in the Velociraptor genus preferred to keep their feet on the ground. Instead of flying, they would **RUN** at speeds up to 25 mph (40 km/h). They always kept their large claw raised off the ground, ready to snatch up prey, which they would then kill with a **BITE**.

Sense of smell.

They had large eyes and thus probably were nocturnal hunters.

Cretaceous
(75 million years ago)

Austroraptor

Claws.

Their rather slender snout indicates that their bite wasn't powerful at all.

Cretaceous
(78 million years ago)

Austroraptor lived in a region that corresponds to South America today. Compared to North American raptors, they had shorter arms and a more elongated snout. They probably used their **CLAWS** to grab small animals or fish, then picked them up with their small conical **TEETH**, which weren't at all suited for tearing flesh.

JURASSIC QUESTIONS

10 QUESTIONS FOR 10 ANIMALS! IF YOU DON'T KNOW THE ANSWERS, THAT'S OK! GIVE THEM A TRY ANYWAY, AND DON'T WORRY ABOUT BEING RIGHT OR WRONG. THEN TURN THE PAGE TO SEE IF YOU GOT THEM RIGHT!

10. HOW DID IGUANODON WALK?

A On two legs

B On four legs

C On both two and four legs

9. WHAT WERE THE PLATES ON STEGOSAURUS'S BACK MADE OF?

A Of bone, like its skeleton

B Of keratin, like its nails

C Of ivory, like its teeth

8. WHAT DOES THE NAME THERIZINOSAURUS MEAN?

A Thunder reptile

B Sickle reptile

C Hammer reptile

7. WHY DID THE ANKYLOSAURUS HAVE SHORT LEGS?

A To more easily eat small plants on the ground

B To walk easily in the undergrowth

C In order to avoid tripping

6. WHAT WAS THE TAIL OF DEINONYCHUS LIKE?

A Long and rigid

B Soft and stretchy

C Robust and flexible

5. WHAT KIND OF NAILS DID APATOSAURUS HAVE?

A Claws

B Hooves

C None at all

4. HOW MANY TEETH DID TRICERATOPS HAVE?

A 200

B 20

C 2

3. HOW LONG COULD AN AVERAGE T. REX HAVE LIVED?

A 16 years

B 28 years

C 64 years

2. WHERE HAVE SPINOSAURUS BONES BEEN FOUND?

A In China

B In Antarctica

C In North Africa

1. WHAT WAS SPECIAL ABOUT TROODON EGGS

A They were laid two by two

B They were brightly colored

C They were the size of a hazelnut

10, C — When just moseying along, they probably walked on their hind legs. But in cases of danger, they would use all four limbs for a super-fast getaway.

9, A — The flat plates arranged in a double row along Stegosaurus's back were made of bone. However, they were not attached directly to the skeleton. Instead, they were embedded in the skin and may have been covered only with keratin.

8, B — The name Therizinosaurus comes from the Greek words *sauros*, meaning "reptile," and *therizo*, which means "scythe." It's a made-up name to emphasize its fearsome claws.

7, C — The belly was the only part of the body not protected by armor, but because of its short legs, it remained close to the ground. During a fight, Ankylosaurus could quickly lie down on the ground to avoid being flipped over by a predator.

6, A
By swinging its tail, Deinonychus could quickly change direction mid-stride without falling.
Its long, rigid tail helped it stay balanced.

5, A
Apatosaurus had large claws on its hands. It probably used them to grab branches and reach for leaves higher up, or to dig in the ground and bury eggs or search for water.

4, A
The mouth of a Triceratops could have had up to 200 teeth! They were arranged in about 40 rows, each of which had 3-5 teeth stacked vertically.
As they grew, the sharp new teeth pushed out the old dull ones.

3, B
This number was hypothesized by some scientists by studying bones, which like tree trunks, sometimes have growth rings.

2, C
Spinosaurus lived in an area that is now in the northern part of the African continent. The landscape must have been very different back then; it was crossed by large rivers carrying a lot of water.

1, A
Female Troodon laid two eggs each day, burying them partly in the mud. Within a little more than a week, there would have been 16 to 24 eggs in her nest, which were then brooded by the male as well.

CRISTINA BANFI

With a degree in natural sciences from the University of Milan, Cristina Banfi has taught at several schools. She has been involved in science communication and education for more than 20 years and has been part of publishing projects in both scholastic and popular fields, particularly for children and young people. In recent years, she has written several books for White Star.

PHOTO CREDITS

All photographs are from Shutterstock except the following:
Alamy Images pages 29 and 34.

Editorial coordination
Giada Francia

Graphic design and layout
Valentina Figus

WSkids
WHITE STAR KIDS

White Star Kids™ is a trademark of White Star s.r.l.

© 2023 White Star s.r.l.
Piazzale Luigi Cadorna, 6 - 20123 Milan, Italy
www.whitestar.it

Translation: Katherine Kirby
Editing: Michele Suchomel-Casey

All rights reserved. No part of this publication may be reproduced, stored or transmitted in any form or by any means without written permission from the publisher.

ISBN 978-88-544-1991-9
2 3 4 5 6 27 26 25 24 23

Printed and manufactured in China
by Dream Colour (Hong Kong) Printing Limited

FSC
www.fsc.org
MIX
Paper from
responsible sources
FSC® C178000